Dangerous Acts Starring Unstable Elements

Dangerous Acts Starring Unstable Elements

HOWIE GOOD

THE POETRY PRESS
Los Angeles   Hollywood

THE POETRY PRESS
OF PRESS AMERICANA
http://www.americanpopularculture.com

Cover Art: Photo courtesy of Matt at publicdomainarchive.com

Library of Congress Cataloging-in-Publication Data

Names: Good, Howie.
Title: Dangerous acts starring unstable elements / Howie Good.
Description: Los Angeles : Poetry Press of Press Americana, 2016. |
  "2015
Identifiers: LCCN 2015035487 | ISBN 9780996777902
Classification: LCC PS3607.O5628 A6 2016 | DDC 811/.6--dc23
LC record available at http://lccn.loc.gov/2015035487

Part I

Part II

Part I

The Destruction Business

Wine froze
on the table,

milk froze
in the cow's

udder.

Russian
has no word

for a parent
who has lost

a child.

Defoe in the Pillory

The curious
watched him
from behind
police barricades.
Someone asked
about sleep.
"Everything takes
forever in my life,"
he declared dramatically,
although his eyes
remained closed.
It was custom to pelt
the condemned
with dung or dead cats.
The rest flung
flowers at his face.

The Unhappy Ape

A man holding a razor.
A man on a chair smoking.
A man shitting.
All quite indifferent
to one another's
presence or plight.

As you walk through
room after room
it becomes clear
that only grimaces remain,
that the worst
has happened,
that you can live
with the worst.

A man sits naked
with torn newspaper
around his feet.
A man reclines in a vest
on a stained red couch.
The bandages and the screams
are already in place.

Man is an unhappy ape.
But if he knows it, he isn't.

Dangerous Acts Starring Unstable Elements (1)

I fell off my bike,
and when I woke up,
I was here, obsessed
with unhealthy carbohydrates,
flickering surfaces,
broken people and animals,
and the way they stand,
and the trouble they get in.

How could anything
bother me on such a day?
I'd barf my brains out
through my eyeballs
for you if I could.

I've always hoped
in a sense to be able
to paint your mouth
like Monet painted a sunset.

The Secret World of Doing Nothing

You press a button
with the palm of your hand
and still fail to disappear.
I have other problems –
X-rays, a pig's red nose,
loads of ghosts and aura.
But what appeals to me
is precisely this difficulty,
thunder fishtailing across the sky,
reckless tittle-tattle,
so many stolen passwords
the dog eavesdrops
while squatting
to do its business.

After Death

In Jewish tradition
a righteous man
is buried with a gross
of prayer books
atop his coffin.

How long it takes
for life to rewind itself!
And the whole time
the gates of the heart
remain grimly closed
against robbers and wolves,
the things one senses,
some combination
of blue and dark green.

When Uncle Lou was buried,
they placed the books
in cardboard boxes
labeled Kitchen Utensils.

Simple Brushstrokes on a Naked Canvas

Someone comes along
with a machine and thinks he's a god,
and I don't need that.

But he's certainly an emperor, a king.
After the war, we see the view
from his left eye as he lies on a chaise longue,
the view out over his moustache.

How terrible. No colors. Green light without colors.
Because a feeling has no form.
It has a blurred quality, a kind of flailing about.

I'll paint it red.
Hundreds of people will line up outside to enter,
although there will be no wait.

I Scream, You Scream

At the end of the Ben & Jerry's factory tour,
a twenty-something in a white lab coat
gave us each a sample of strawberry rhubarb ice cream.
This flavor, she kept repeating, isn't sold in stores.
I told her I went to Hebrew school with Jerry.
He was also in my homeroom in junior high school
(our last names – Good, Greenfield – both begin with G).
Awesome, she said, though she may not have believed me.
The strawberry rhubarb tasted just OK.

Perspective

Is it normal to be able to see
your veins through your skin?
she asks the doctor,

& no one even answers,
not Miss Navajo, or the house guests,
or the sun-beaten path,

that it's about yearning,
it's about words
& the spaces between words,

a chorus of yips & hoots,
the bones made visible,
what you trip over when you step back
to take in the view.

All Is Straw

My heart is crying, crying…
Rather to blow up, then!
Let's be wild tonight.
Roses plural or Rose's roses
with an apostrophe?
It is hovering and it's not an aircraft.
Dear me! I think I'm turning into a god.
Oh wow. Oh wow. Oh wow.

NB: Based on "Last Words" at Wikiquotes, available at
http://en.wikiquote.org/wiki/Last_words

The Culture Industry Reconsidered

It was like being locked up
inside a Golden Book for children,
black-and-white cows
wherever we looked,
and all wore blue hairnets,
but then someone said
that they're only animals,
that their laughter
was a mockery of happiness,
an agglomeration of vats,
pipes, ventilators, and chutes,
until I hardly knew
what really went on
between hand and metal,
and adulthood came
to mean being old enough
to get the electric chair
if you shot a man in Texas.

At the Sculpture Garden

And what's this supposed to be?
A gazebo for two anarchists?
An aluminum replica of a beehive?
Mozart's birthday?

It eludes me, but we stand there
on the side of the hill, holding hands
and looking expectantly around,
like any other older couple waiting for a UFO.

Storm King

My God!
This is an awful place.
Shadows and dust

and women
in their private chambers
being ravaged
by bird men.

Three ovals soar,
eyes of the sky.

I begin to shake
at the falling
of the first dim flakes.

No one else
seems to remember
the proclamation
that writing poetry
after Auschwitz is barbaric.

And the youngest,
staggering along
against a background
of alleys and vacant lots,

dream of living the life
that faded, dead butterflies
pinned in a cabinet did.

Bitter Sky

Just then it starts raining.
Silently I compare the sound to a torso
being cut with razors and scalpel.
The news this week is full of stories from the famine zone.
Next week, who knows?
Screaming seahorses? Meat confetti? Bitter sky?
If no one tries to answer the question, no one can be wrong.
In the background are five men,
seventeen days, one wall, fifteen boulders.

In Case of Emergency

It was like trying to tell time by a clock without numbers
or hands. I opened the door, and a man was flailing
at the flames with a towel. I almost shut the door again,
but, instead, I did what I figured you'd probably do –
stood there, not quite absorbing everything I was seeing,
and listened for the sirens that would never come.

The Shadow Aspect

They found her
still holding the knife,

as there wasn't
room in her head
for one thing more,

not even a small list
of natural remedies –

ginger for nausea,
plantain for colds,
rose hips for heartache.

Decay of the Aura

I go on various social media
and search for suggestions
about how to still be productive
while extremely depressed.

It's not just the feral cats,
but they aren't helping.
Earthquakes keep happening.

We should have fucked
when we had the chance.

Post-Mambo

You, naked,
an orchid
in the land
of technology,
the secret
to the perfect
something,

although
I didn't
necessarily
want it
that way,

Spanish
dancers
composed
of particles
& waves
leading us
up the street
when,

outside
a drab
forbidding
door,

the blood
of birds
points
skyward

Char & Ash

The history that began
with a signed urinal
was extinguished
with rain disasters in India.

Somewhere I still have
a picture postcard
from the gift shop
at Kafka's birthplace.

Nostalgia just isn't
what it used to be.

Panics keep happening,
followed swiftly
by lewd gestures.

There was a time
when the pullout couch
at your parents'
would have served
as enough of a haven,

even with you & me
& everyone else
crying, Squish over!

Fire Is the Other Animal

I live in the reign
of sparrows

Bird tracks
make circles
in my palms

What isn't is

We have left
bones in the forest
& dark swans
under the water

A collage based on Heather S.J. Steglia, *Water Runs To What Is Wet*
(Burning Deck, 1980)

Revising Thoreau

Thoreau
only left
the woods,
his face
shaded
by a wide hat,
to borrow
a pencil
but found out
there was
a fire
downtown
& stayed
to watch.

Now,
whenever
there's
an interesting bird,
he dashes
outside
& shoots it.

Question #33

Where would you like to be in 10 years?
It's a standard interview question
and deserves a standard response.
Discussing lamb chops, I answer.
The interviewer nods as if he understands.
I have a presentiment that the two ee's
in "feeling" have begun to coagulate.
The best thing for me to do under such circumstances
is repeat a Russian proverb (in English, of course)
and then go look for an open video store.
By the time I return my widowed 89-year-old father
has decided to become someone else,
though still complaining that I don't visit often enough.

The Cruelest Animal

Can't seem
to get things
in focus?

Some of us
never can.

We collide
with pieces
of furniture
& fall over
objects,

& may even
try to walk
through a wall
or a closed door
on the way
from one room
to another.

The worst off
describe people
around them
who, in fact,
aren't there,

but who still
somehow leave
a dead cow
on a piano.

Still Missing

It's when you're trying
to talk about God
and you don't know how
that you discover
another city is possible,

where the only facts
that exist, exist
as incidental music
from forgotten movies,

or as retweets
of movie quotes (e.g.,
"The life of a repo man
is always intense").

Even whales
drink milk there,
and the statue
of John the Baptist
outside a church
searches in the bushes
for his missing head.

An Uncommitted Crime

We stop in front of the stained glass
of Abraham raising the knife.
Who is that, you ask, *Elijah*?

The exhibit goes on
for another five white, sterile rooms.
Behind every work of art
lies an uncommitted crime,
Abraham grasping Isaac's hair.
It's the season's hottest trend,
an ongoing crisis of representation,
populated by ghosts & old men.

I have a hole in my head
I want you to fill with a tongue kiss.

Another Word For It

A naked woman,
pollen caught
in her black fuzz,
stands atop a heap
of broken stones
in a strange pose,

& it's impossible
when looking up at her
not to imagine
some prior tragedy
in a crowded street

or to speak
without whispering,
even if no one
is there to overhear
your obscure,
anxious message.

On Being Asked, "Where Do You Get Your Ideas?"

Nothing here,
and no one,

only seashells
and pebbles
and pretty ferry lights

casting shadows
that form a sentence.

27 Signs You Are in an Existential Crisis

The process is one of clinging
to stained fragments floating around –

a woman taking off her shirt,
the Spanish Armada, an ugly mood,

an eye – and tying them together.

Yet nothing is ever resolved,
nothing adds up, nothing goes anywhere.

I have a box full of photographs
I have taken of clouds to prove it.

Painted by Sheet Lightning

I felt as if saints in angry red robes
were clamoring inside my head.
Who invented disco? I began to ask,
obviously in the wrong language.
The next day brought the person
I want to be (or at least be seen as)
& the other person I keep on being.
Nod if you understand when I say
the rider guides the horse, though only
in the direction the horse wants to go.

Other Bad Omens

I raised up on my toes
to get a better view
& saw that stupid shits
were everywhere.

The 911 operator
suggested calling back
if it happened again,

the sense of having
quotation marks
around all the things
that make me, me.

Night flooded in,
& I was amazed
that there was
such a lot blood
for such a little cut.

The Heavy Shadow of Prior Encounters

I keep my voice low,
like a spy passing secrets.

When they ask my name,
address, date of birth,
I answer as if answering
might mean something.

Somewhere near here
there must be a leaden sea
and someone unknown
to me walking beside it,

carrying a blank page
for the lives I'll never lead.

299 792 458 m / s

The victims were granted
an unconditional right to scream,
their shrill operatic voices
startling birds off roofs & ledges,

& then light began to lose speed,
& from my seat on the train,
I saw Jupiter's four largest moons,
wildflowers flicker & fade,
walls of faces alternating with hills of rubble,
a dog fully clothed walking alone,

& for a moment, maybe longer,
whatever that red toy trumpet, my heart,
said was true was true.

Nausea

WebMD won't tell you how to heal a flapping voice,
a sweaty tongue, the toxicity of speech.
Swish your mouth with something intangible,
the crooked thoughts of a leafless tree.
It isn't just the roads that are bad.
The longtime twilight sky itches & burns.
Sartre's last words were, *I failed.*

Hummingbird

Quick,
come here,
before
it flies away,

a needle-
beaked
amphetamine

hovering
outside
the window

in a dazzle
of wings,

a sort of
blurry
stillness,

practically
silence,

from another
world,

the blue
café

where
Van Gogh
decided

to cut off
his ear.

Dangerous Acts Starring Unstable Elements (2)

Poe liked
to wander
around
cemeteries,
a city now
mostly
abandoned.

Sometimes
he'd be
mistaken
for a battered
woman

and then
hastily
dragged
away
by the
police.

When
he died,
tangled
in a clear
plastic
sheet,

only four
people
attended
his funeral.

The
Germans
have
a word
for this.

Autumn Equinox

A swirling cloud of dust & gravel
sweeps along the ground,
& before I have time to develop
a plausible theory about it,

the woman staggers up to me,
an eye missing, a hand gone,
a brittle blue flower tucked saucily
behind her remaining ear,
& I suddenly know of what the future consists:

a certain unrest in all there has been,

the desire to rescue scrap
& then serve celebratory champagne
to saints & alcoholics,

an unpremeditated encounter
at the breakfast table with an apple, pears,
a heart cut with a cake knife.

The New Normal

It can become tiresome,
all this point, counterpoint.
Nobody seems to realize
we should eat nothing but clouds.
Linger someplace too long
and contexts begin collapsing.
I'm sailing with the rockslide,
a crumbling yellow moon.
I'll be back by my next birthday,
attractive, hip, cradling a lamb,
the lamb looking a little uncomfortable.

Hiking Mount Severance

The higher we climbed,
the hastier the sun became,

& the dry, hacking cough
of traffic still reached us
despite our being besieged by trees,

the leaves outlined in gold
& acetylene, & wavering
like the pale-skinned shadows
of half-created things.

Part II

Buddha & Co.

Exposure has eroded the face of the garden Buddha. Perhaps I shouldn't compare, but Kanye West broke down and cried during a BBC interview. It sounded like treachery, the Dreyfus court martial, Van Gogh getting most of his teeth pulled. And that hadn't happened before. His message was simply, "Your egg, my semen, we change the world." Someone else once said that to feel like an underwater jellyfish is to experience a higher mode of being. Let's cover the walls with soft, plush things, then make people sit on the floor.

My Life and Medieval Times

There's a new exhibit at the museum. Many odd items are on display – hair from the heads of madmen, baby clothes that were worn by a miniature pinscher, a jar of eyeball jelly. Those of us waiting in line avoid any discussion of what is art. It's like watching TV without the sound. The real content lies elsewhere, perhaps with the falcons that invented a whole new language just to preserve their secrets.

Wheatfield With Crows

It was a Sunday, four days before Christmas. He presented himself at licensed brothel no. 1, asked for a girl named Rachel, and handed her his ear (or, more precisely, the lower part of his left ear) as if it were a small painting of a wheatfield with crows. "Guard this object carefully," he said. Then he disappeared. The blood showed up as black in the black-and-white news photos.

Collage

The most difficult stage is filling the last space. Everything gives the appearance of something that is absent. Atomic clouds linger in a kind of faceless brooding, skyscrapers burn without leaving a visible mark. You can't even see the wind blowing as there's nothing for it to touch or move. It's a circular path into nowhere. Spiraling, even. Beneath a twelfth-century sky yellow with age, clerks of nostalgia gather shattered pieces, the latest of which is a Madonna in peacock feathers.

The Part I Don't Get

Whichever phone number I call, the suicide hotline rings. That's the part I don't get. Then the scene changes – a burned girl, about 10, hooked up to a morphine drip. Off in the distance, skyscrapers loom through 9/11 dust. I have no plans, and no secrets either. A camera is being developed for satellites that can view facial expressions from space. But don't worry. The government can't constitutionally use it yet. And unless you live somewhere sunny, they can't see you anyway.

The Penalty for Trying

It's not true that there's no penalty for trying. Van Gogh was locked up in the madhouse in Arles for touching the local women. Only yesterday, a man passing through the train paused beside my seat and asked where I was going, and a few minutes later, there he was again with the same rotten crumbling teeth. Everything that wasn't water was fire. The police wore brown uniforms; the soldiers, black. I soon gave up all hope of falling back asleep, though the locomotive in my dream continued burning.

A Project Called "Nothing"

An older couple stood off to the side with their bags and electronic devices. Around them, wisps of primary colors lay on the floor. "This is wrong," she said, using a small mirror as a guide. I had a vision of her carving a star into her stomach with a razor and screaming until her voice gave out. Then one night, in the middle of the night, I woke up thinking: "It's not that I'm doing nothing. It's just that there is nothing." And so now, at about 6 p.m. every day, I lock the empty rooms with a key.

Remote

It never happens, tomorrow never happens, the movie
gangster says, more to himself than to his double-crossing
partner, who isn't listening anyway and wouldn't understand
the concept of built-in obsolescence even if he were. In the
news clip Ukrainians – or are they Iranians? – shake
automatic weapons over their heads. The contestant on
another channel is struggling to remember the name of the
fourth Beatle. At least he knows you must state the answer
as a question, which only proves, I guess, that the heart was
and still is A) a highway B) a jailhouse C) an empty bed.

Words Fail Me

The moon huddled in the farthest corner of the sky. A slutty teen bobbed her head up and down, up and down. The dream of flying had come of age. It was either that or stay home. I made a list of things still to do: choke, weave, sense, deal, blunder. Which left just enough time to admire, between small, tedious breaths, the snowy egret standing there.

Objects in This Mirror

If they ask what it all means, answer, *When*? And if they persist, just point, and not with your finger. Point with your tongue at the old-fashioned girl in the Mao cap who abhors the politics but loves the poetry of Ezra Pound. Point with your eyelashes at the tournament of events that objects undergo. Point with your fading heart at the shadows puddled in the bottom of the ditch, where, nonetheless, something still glitters like the blue velvet and gilt doghouse made for one of Marie Antoinette's puppies.

"Admiration Is the Emotion Furthest From Understanding"

Admire the Japanese beetle, luminescent green racing stripe between its bombazine wings / admire the sky, shredded and fading, like the eyesight of a syphilitic / admire the woman from HR who drowned herself while on vacation / admire everyday objects – brown beer bottles, metronomes, gas fireplaces – some with only one good eye, some with a dog's heart / admire the phenomenon represented by the word "glint" / admire the refugee writer Theodor Adorno, though that wasn't his real name / admire the stuttering silence that we pretend, for the public's sake, suffices.

Epic

I have already somehow survived childhood, a nervous breakdown, and smart phones. Being a misunderstood, isolated creature opens up a certain aspect of time. Balloon Pop Outlaw Black, let's say. The rescuing angel, seeing things as they are, leaves town, eyes in a mask with puffed-up cheeks. Others, kneeling like supplicants to avoid drowning, weed around the base of the watchtower, their concentration insistently challenged by the noise and fumes of the flaming chariot that roars back and forth through the canary yellow suburbs of night.

Just a Theory

Whatever is obsolete is free for the taking, the unfit on the outskirts of the herd, easy meals for wild dogs and hyenas. It came to me while waiting in the express lane (a serious misnomer!) at the supermarket. I was studying the covers of *Us Weekly* and *People*, even though none of the names in megawatt rainbow lettering were familiar, or their disembodied faces either. Did I mention I have a theory that the breakup of Martin and Lewis was a function of rising Cold War tensions? Pointless weirdness gets old fast, but sometimes I can't help myself. Buddy Holly looked right at my mother at the show in Duluth three days before the plane crash.

Relics of Narrative Progression

I wake up in a hotel room in Murder City, bullets of rain exploding against the window. There may be a strange woman in my bed, or there may not. It all depends on which movie we're in. I look in the mirror and see that I still have the same face, deep, dark grooves around dead eyes. Down in the street, dangerous men in leather trench coats are waiting for me to come out. I have no plan. It's a story without plot, less a story than a set of cryptic symptoms. Some would consider this a failing. I consider it merely a collection of words – thunderstorms, chandelier, Blythe Danner, ocean.

Bureaucratic Pathologies

Is it winter there where you are? Do you have a dancing monkey to help you get through it? I can't close my eyes without dreaming that they have taken my shoelaces and belt away and that I'm calmly being interrogated by the torturer's horse under a biblically threatening sky. When I return to work in the morning, someone has posted photocopies of a photo of child soldiers all around the office. My new office-mate is old enough to have been a Nazi death camp guard. *If you want something to happen*, he says, smiling, *just act like you don't and then maybe it will.*

Bergasse 19

The sexperts say it's Freud who established the great emporium, a sort of museum of human misery, with parents and broken dolls and old crumbling shadows arranged according to unknown laws. By coincidence, you're visiting a city that claims to be Kafka's birthplace, his name, or something that at least looks like it, carved on the trees. As you act the tourist throughout the afternoon, De Kooning's women, all pink flesh and piranha teeth, rear up around you. What was so difficult to understand was the message to "Please call."

Every Everything

The needle goes in / never pausing to narrate / just like the
9-year-old at Joy Farm firing an Uzi / the pretty young
maidens / eat a pear in the French manner / jamming a fork
in the top / & cutting chunks from the sides / the ghostly
traces of a past life / every day for three years / drawing new
maps of hell / in the French manner / intimately / with a
scalpel / & he who says doesn't know / & she who knows
doesn't say / that once it goes in / it never comes out

Angelus

I began this fall by watching a thin red squirrel it would be worth it to go ninety miles out of your way to see. So what shall we do about this angel, broken wing on the left? The smell of piss is what. When I woke up this morning I knew there was horror. It will always be invisible, it will. My friends, still of this world, follow me to the bottom of the river. Suddenly there are hundreds of fishermen on the road.

A collage based on Gerald Stern, *The Red Coal* (Houghton Mifflin, 1981)

Blues Chords

Ask anyone. Ask an undertaker. Ask him about roses growing out of people's brains, alligators crawling through sewers, lovers turning into graveyard angels, souped-up cars running full blast on a Friday night, the so-called "old, weird America," a haze of shadows drifting in the open window, where I move to the movements of the naked woman slip-sliding under me, our flesh, inside & out, zebra-striped at hundreds of miles per second.

Academe (A Fable)

When deer invaded the Humanities Building, singly and in pairs, a chaos of white-tailed shadows, the university police (in bulletproof vests!) rushed to the roof to escape the vicious clatter of hooves, and all the deans and all their assistants screamed from the upper windows for the proper forms to be filled out, while down in my suddenly empty classroom, I could feel through the floor the shudder of a nameless longing for something that doesn't exist.

A Fairy Tale

Somewhere near here a boy and his twin sister have taken the wrong trail. The notion of time just got harder to understand. In what seems like a sign of some sort, light drains from the sky, and the wind begins counting backwards. Soon it's completely dark, with no way to know whether it's the frightened mouth, or the stranger's hand clamped over it, that's most like a dead rose.

Dark Victory

No one had ever told us what would happen in the event of defeat. Then the crows showed up, sometimes alone, more often in pairs and small groups. At least one man in attendance regarded it as a baleful omen. The rest assumed that it was just a blip. But, very soon, antediluvian gods faded into rain, the flickering surface of uproarious dreams.

Film

It was about a retired schoolteacher, a short, balding man who looked a little like Eichmann. Even after living there for years, he still referred to himself as a tourist. The beggar woman squatting in the doorway smiled at him, revealing several missing teeth. Two brothers, one in rough wool pants whose Hebrew name meant wolf, one with a small sack slung over his shoulder whose Hebrew name meant laughter, tramped in and out. The sky acquired a touch of red. We felt raindrops, tiny, struggling things.

And That's What It's All About

There is no number one. This makes me feel better. That's part of the mystery. Punished children have their heads replaced by apples. A sacrilegious saint puffs a Lucky Strike in benediction over a nude torso. Nasty stains of every imaginable kind, the memorabilia of a witless age, constitute another wing of the museum. If you stare, the blood-stained figure stares back, daring you to ask what it's like to be Googled. You turn your face away, and through the window, glimpse debris – a small empty flowerpot, an erection lasting longer than four hours, used DVDs, Vienna during the Nazi period, those kinds of things. Suddenly you're doing something else, afraid even to go to sleep due to the overwhelming fear of waking up.

Police State 2.0

An unknown person or persons (excuse the jargon) entered the offices of the Minister of Drought, opened the safes and files, and wiped the baby's chin, after which a special investigator was appointed, grimacing like a bust of Beethoven, only to discover that a lapse in the space-time continuum may be a theoretical possibility, but not something that has actually happened, and even if it did, the teenagers in the first few cars of the plunging roller coaster would still be laughing.

Flag of Skin

The sky ripples like the eerie back of a burly man. I am beginning to dread Thursdays, with their unreliable forecasts. Let's take the escalator to the basement and avoid the escaped killers possibly hiding among the dark, lean shrubs. You can bring the music of the neighborhood birds. I can bring my watered-down Zen philosophies. Just follow the guests from the wedding from which the beautiful young bride long ago fled.

Acknowledgments

The author wishes to thank the editors of the following publications in which some of the poems in this book originally appeared, sometimes in different form: 1947: A Literary Journal, The 2River View, Bluepepper, Construction Magazine, Counterpunch, Epigraphs, Future Trading, Hardly Donuts, Hermeneutic Chaos Literary Journal, Hollow Publishing, Ithacalit, Potluck, New Bourgeois, New Verse News, Noble / Gas QTRLY, One Sentence Poems, Otoliths, Poetry WTF?!, The Purple Pig, Ppigpenn, Red Booth Review, Red Ceilings, Review Americana, Right Hand Pointing, Smashed Cake, Star 82 Review, Uut Poetry, and Zoomozophone.

Author Bio

Howie Good, a journalism professor at SUNY New Paltz, is the author of several poetry collections, including *Beautiful Decay* and *The Cruel Radiance of What Is* from Another New Calligraphy, *Fugitive Pieces* from Right Hand Pointing Press, and *Lovesick* from The Poetry Press of Press Americana. He co-edits White Knuckle Press with Dale Wisely.

9 780996 777902